Worship

The Lutheran Difference Series

Steven Mueller

Contributions by

Edward Engelbrecht

CONCORDIA PUBLISHING HOUSE · SAINT LOUIS

Written by Steven Mueller, contributions by Edward Engelbrecht

Edited by Robert Baker and Edward Engelbrecht

This publication may be available in braille, in large print, or on cassette tape for the visually impaired. Please allow 8 to 12 weeks for delivery. Write to the Library for the Blind, 1333 S. Kirkwood Road, St. Louis, MO 63122-7295; call 1-800-433-3954, ext. 1322; or e-mail to blind.library@lcms.org.

Contents

About This Series

"I'm having trouble understanding you Lutherans."

"Why's that?"

"Well, you preach and pray like Baptists but your worship services are just like the Roman Catholics."

"I've always thought our worship tradition was unique."

"Well, why should tradition matter at all? Shouldn't we just follow the Bible?"

As Lutherans interact with other Christians, they often find themselves struggling to explain their beliefs and practices. Although many Lutherans have learned the "what" of the doctrines of the church, they do not always have a full scriptural foundation to share the "why." When confronted with different doctrines, they cannot clearly state their faith, much less understand the differences between denominations.

Because of insecurities about explaining particular doctrines or practices, some Lutherans may avoid opportunities to share what they have learned from Christ and His Word. The Lutheran Difference Bible study series will identify how Lutherans differ from other Christians and demonstrate from the Bible why Lutherans differ. These studies will prepare Lutherans to share their faith and help non-Lutherans understand the Lutheran difference.

An Overview of Christian Denominations

The following outline of Christian history will help you understand where the different denominations come from and how they are related to one another. Use this outline in connection with the "Comparisons" sections found throughout the study. Statements of belief for the different churches are drawn from their official confessional writings.

The Great Schism

Eastern Orthodox: On July 16, 1054, Cardinal Humbert entered the Cathedral of the Holy Wisdom in Constantinople just before the worship service. He stepped to the altar and left a letter condemning Michael Cerularius, patriarch of Constantinople. Cerularius responded by condemning the letter and its authors. In that moment, the Christian churches of the east and west were severed from one another. Their disagreements centered on what bread could be used in the Lord's Supper and the addition of the filioque statement (see glossary, p. 79) to the Nicene Creed.

The Reformation

Lutheran: On June 15, 1520, Pope Leo X wrote a letter condemning Dr. Martin Luther for his Ninety-five Theses. Luther's theses had challenged the sale of indulgences, a fund-raising effort to pay for the building of St. Peter's Cathedral in Rome. The letter charged Luther with heresy and threatened to excommunicate him if he did not retract his writings within 60 days. Luther replied by publicly burning the letter. Leo excommunicated him on January 3, 1521, and condemned all who agreed with Luther or supported his cause.

Reformed: In 1522 the preaching of Ulrich Zwingli in Zurich, Switzerland, convinced people to break their traditional Lenten fast. Also, Zwingli preached that priests should be allowed to marry. When local friars challenged these departures from medieval church practice, the Zurich Council supported Zwingli and agreed that the Bible should guide Christian doctrine and practice. Churches of this Reformed tradition include Presbyterians and Episcopalians.

Anabaptist: In January 1525 Conrad Grebel, a follower of Ulrich Zwingli, rebaptized Georg Blaurock. Blaurock began rebaptizing others and founded the Swiss Brethren. Their insistence on adult believers' Baptism distinguished them from other churches of the Reformation. Anabaptists attracted social extremists who advocated violence in the cause of Christ, complete pacifism, or communal living. Mennonite, Brethren, and Amish churches descend from this movement.

The Counter Reformation

Roman Catholic: When people call the medieval church "Roman Catholic," they make a common historical mistake. Roman Catholicism as we know it emerged after the Reformation. As early as 1518 Luther and other reformers had appealed to the pope and requested a council to settle the issue of indulgences. Their requests were hindered or denied for a variety of theological and political reasons. Finally, on December 13, 1545, 34 leaders from the churches who opposed the Reformation gathered at the invitation of Pope Paul III. They began the Council of Trent (1545–63), which established the doctrine and practice of Roman Catholicism.

Post-Reformation Movements

Baptist: In 1608 or 1609 John Smyth, a former pastor of the Church of England, baptized himself by pouring water over his head. He formed a congregation of English Separatists in Holland, who opposed the rule of bishops and infant Baptism. This marked the start of the English Baptist churches, which remain divided doctrinally over the theology of John Calvin (Particular Baptists) and Jacob Arminius (General Baptists). In the 1800s the Restoration Movement of Alexander Campbell, a former Presbyterian minister, adopted many Baptist teachings. These churches include the Disciples of Christ (Christian Churches) and the Churches of Christ.

Wesleyan: In 1729 John and Charles Wesley gathered with three other men to study the Scripture, receive Communion, and discipline one another according to the "method" laid down in the Bible. Later, John Wesley's preaching caused religious revivals in England and America. Methodists, Wesleyans, Nazarenes, and Pentecostals form the Wesleyan family of churches.

A special note needs to be added about Pentecostalism, the most recent branch in the Wesleyan family. On January 1, 1901 Agnes Ozman, Charles Parham (a former Methodist Episcopal minister), and others experienced the "Pentecost blessing" (including speaking in "tongues" or "glossolalia"). Further "baptisms" in the Holy Spirit took place at Azusa Street in Los Angeles, California (1906). Pentecostal worship emphasizes impulsive responses to the Holy Spirit. In addition to "tongues," Pentecostals seek miraculous healings, prophecies, and other signs of the Spirit's power. Worship usually involves repeated phrases, progressively faster musical tempos, and changes in musical keys to evoke emotional responses. Today, there are more than 300 Pentecostal denominations and associations in North America, making it one of the most divided Christian groups.

Liberal: In 1799 Friedrich Schleiermacher published *Addresses on Religion* in an attempt to make Christianity appealing to people influenced by rationalism. He argued that religion is not a body of doctrines, provable truths, or a system of ethics, but belongs to the realm of feelings. His ideas did not lead to the formation of a new denomination, but deeply influenced Christian thinking. Denominations most thoroughly affected by liberalism are the United Church of Christ, Disciples of Christ, and Unitarianism.

Lutheran Facts

All who worship the Holy Trinity and trust in Jesus Christ for the forgiveness of sins are regarded by Lutherans as fellow Christians, despite denominational differences.

Lutheran churches first described themselves as *evangelische*, or evangelical, churches. Opponents of these churches called them *Lutheran* after Dr. Martin Luther, the sixteenth-century German church reformer.

Lutherans are not disciples of Dr. Martin Luther, but rather are disciples of Jesus Christ. They proudly accept the name *Lutheran* because they agree with Dr. Luther's teaching from the Bible, as summarized in Luther's Small Catechism.

Lutherans are led in worship by a pastor.

The service follows an *order*, an outline of worship that addresses spiritual needs such as forgiveness, edification, and spiritual nurture.

Lutheran orders of service are from the western (Latin) liturgical tradition. This stems from the synagogue and temple worship practiced by the earliest Christians, who were Jewish.

The Lutheran Reformation restored the practice of congregational singing, which had largely disappeared during the Middle Ages. The Lutheran church has been called "the singing church."

Lutheran *chorales* spread to every nation touched by the Reformation. The chorales stem from the simple congregational songs of the early Middle Ages (Gregorian chant or plainsong).

Lutheran hymns have typically focused on the gracious work of the Holy Trinity for our salvation.

To prepare for "The God We Worship," read Exodus 20:1–8.

The God We Worship

Surely my heart cannot truly rest, nor be entirely contented, unless it rest in Thee.

Thomas a Kempis

What first comes to mind when you think of worship? Possibly your thoughts are of a church service, a prayer, a sermon, or a song. Perhaps you think of a certain building. Maybe a discussion that you've had with another Christian over worship forms or styles comes to mind. Chances are that your first reaction is on something that we do or are involved in when we worship.

1. What are your first reactions to the word "worship"?

Were the items given above, or your first thoughts good examples of where our focus should lie? Worship needs to be focused on God and His Word.

2. Was God part of your first reaction? If not, why do you think this is so?

Why Worship?

3. Read Psalm 29, Psalm 145:3 and Revelation 5:12. According to these verses, why should we worship God?

4. Look at Exodus 20:8 and Hebrews 10:25. What reasons for worship do these passages provide?

5. In the Small Catechism, Martin Luther wrote that the third commandment means, "We should fear and love God so that we do not despise preaching and His Word, but hold it sacred and gladly hear and learn it." How does this help to focus our understanding of the commandment?

6. Worship isn't simply a set of activities to do or words to speak. Worship needs an object. We are to worship God. In the explanation to the first commandment in *The Large Catechism*, Luther writes, "A god means that from which we are to expect all good and to which we are to take refuge in all distress, so that to have [the One] God is nothing else than to trust and believe Him from the whole heart." According to this definition, what is your god? Is there anyone who doesn't have a god?

7. If we are to worship the true God, we must know who He is. What do Deuteronomy 6:4 and Matthew 28:19 show us about the nature of the true God?

8. There are many people in our world who deny the doctrine of the Trinity, and yet still claim to worship God. What does Jesus say about this in John 14:6? How does 1 Corinthians 12:3 also expand our understanding?

9. The triune God is worthy of our worship. Does anything or anyone else deserve or rightly receive our worship? See Isaiah 42:8 and Revelation 22:8–9.

True Worship

10. We have looked at a number of different things necessary for true worship. Briefly summarize what we have seen. If these things are necessary for true worship, have we ever engaged in false worship? If so, how should we respond?

11. In the Athanasian Creed we confess, "the catholic [i.e. universal] faith is this, that we worship one God in Trinity, and Trinity in Unity." Notice that the Creed doesn't just say we *believe* in the Trinity, but that we *worship* the Trinity. How does this help us understand the nature of worship?

12. We have looked at several reasons for worship. What things particularly move you to worship?

One Triune God

13. Read Exodus 20:1–8, which is commonly known as the *first table of the Law*. What common element do you see in each of the commandments and their place in the list of Ten Commandments? How does Jesus summarize them in Matthew 22:37?

14. Reflect carefully on the liturgy and music used at church. What affirmations do you note that the Holy Trinity is the true God?

15. How might you invite someone to come worship with you this week? How might you introduce them to the true God, so that they may receive His blessings?

Comparisons

The term creed comes from the Latin word *credo*, "I believe." Creeds are summary confessions of faith used by the vast majority of Christians. They developed at a time when most people could not read and needed a memorable rule of faith. The root of creeds is found in reciting the *shema* in ancient Judaism as part of daily prayer. The *shema* is drawn from Deuteronomy 6:4–9, 11, 13–21 and Numbers 15:37–41. It served as a summary of biblical teaching and was probably recited by Jesus and the apostles. (See Mark 12:28–31, where Jesus recites a portion of the *shema* to answer a teacher of the Law.)

After Jesus ascended into heaven, the earliest Christians began using summaries of Christian teaching (e.g., see 1 Corinthians 15:3–5). These summaries developed into the creeds listed below:

Apostles' Creed. A summary which began to take shape already at the time of the apostles. This creed developed from a series of questions asked of a person at the time of Baptism. History shows that congregations in Rome were using a form of this creed in the second century but the wording did not receive its standard form until much later. Most churches from the western (Latin) tradition still use the Apostles' Creed for instruction and as a confession of faith in worship.

Nicene Creed. A summary of Christian teaching adopted by congregations of the Roman Empire at the council of Nicaea in 325. The creed was expanded by the council of Constantinople in

381 to help settle other Christological controversies of the fourth century. Today, Eastern Orthodox churches and most churches from the western (Latin) tradition confess the Nicene creed in worship, especially during a communion service. In the Middle Ages, the western churches added the *filioque* statement (see glossary, p. 79).

Athanasian Creed. A longer creed addressing the Christological controversies of the fourth and fifth centuries. It is named for Athanasius (c. 296–373), the bishop of Alexandria, who vigorously opposed Arianism. However, Athanasius did not write this creed, since it emerged much later. Many churches of the western (Latin) tradition use the Athanasian Creed. Lutheran congregations typically recite it on Trinity Sunday. The creed has been included in Eastern Orthodox services, minus the *filioque* statement.

No creed but the Bible. Congregations of the Restoration movement rejected the use of creeds early in the nineteenth century. They taught that creeds divided Christians from one another and agreement on the Bible as God's Word was a sufficient basis for unity. Christian Churches, Disciples of Christ, and Churches of Christ descend from this movement.

Pseudo-Christian Beliefs. A variety of groups reject the doctrine of the Trinity. For example, the Jehovah's Witnesses regard Jesus as a created god and the Holy Spirit as an impersonal force. The United Pentecostal Church teaches that the Father, Son, and Holy Spirit are all manifestations of the same person ("Jesus only"). Mormons hold that the Holy Spirit is a spiritual god alongside the Father and the Son, who are gods with physical bodies.

Liturgical churches (Eastern Orthodox, Lutheran, Reformed, Roman Catholic, and some Wesleyans) regularly recite a creed during their worship services. Many nonliturgical churches accept the teachings of the creeds but do not use them in their worship services.

Point to Remember

You shall have no other gods before me. . . . You shall not misuse the name of the LORD your God . . . Remember the Sabbath day by keeping it holy. Exodus 20:3, 7–8

To prepare for "The People Who Worship," read John 4:19–26.

The People Who Worship

God wishes us to believe Him and to receive from Him blessings, and this He declares to be true divine service.

Philip Melanchthon, Apology of the Augsburg Confession III:107

Driving home from worship one Sunday morning, Susan pondered Pastor Gomez's sermon. He drew a connection between the Gospel reading and their community in a way she had not considered before. Intrigued, she asked her family what they thought of the message. Her question was met with an awkward silence. When she pressed further, it seemed that no one else had listened to the sermon. "Come on, Mom," her son complained, "isn't it enough that we went to church?"

16. How would you respond to the son's question?

17. Are you ever tempted to think of worship as something to attend and watch, but not really participate in? Why does this happen?

In Spirit and Truth

18. In John 4, Jesus talks with a Samaritan woman who had led a sad and sinful life. When His questions get too personal, she tries to distract Him with a question on worship. Read John 4:19–26. What does she ask? How does Jesus respond? What do you think it means to "worship in spirit"?

19. How does the opening quote on page 16 reflect Jesus' teaching?

20. Many of our worship services begin with Confession and Absolution. Read 1 John 1:8–9 and Psalm 32:5. Why are Confession and Absolution important preparation for worship?

21. In John 4:23–24, Jesus told the woman that true worshipers worship in spirit. What else did He teach her? What does it mean to "worship in truth"? See also John 17:17.

22. Sometimes, Christians speak as if this emphasis on "spirit and truth" is unique to the New Testament. Read Hosea 6:6. How does this passage reflect this same teaching?

23. Hosea calls us to a living faith. Read Romans 12:1. What does this verse call us to do? What is our motivation for this? How can we do this?

By Faith Alone

24. Seeing this biblical teaching on worship, is it ever proper for us to consider worship simply as "going through the motions," or

mindlessly repeating words or actions? What can we do to avoid these problems?

25. Every religion in the world has some form of worship. Most of the members of these religions seem sincere and many seem to live good lives. Without faith in Christ, are they engaged in true worship?

26. God reveals Himself to us and calls us to worship Him. How should we relate to those who do not acknowledge Him or worship Him? See 1 Peter 3:15.

Taking Stock

27. We have seen how our worship is rightly preceded by confession and absolution. Read Matthew 6:11–12. What hint do these words of Jesus contain about how often we should pray? How often we should ask for forgiveness?

28. In our introduction, we saw Susan talking with her family about worship. Write below the name of a family member or a friend with whom you could talk about worship this week. What blessings might you describe for them from the Divine Service? How does God speak to you in His Word? How does He nourish and nurture your faith?

Comparisons

Christians have typically defined their doctrine of worship under the doctrine of the church and ministry.

Eastern Orthodox: "What is to be noted of the *place* where the Liturgy is celebrated? It must always be consecrated in a *temple*, the *table* in which, or at least, if there be no such table, the *antimense* [altar cloth] on which the Sacrament is consecrated, must have been consecrated by a Bishop. Why is the *temple* called a *church?* Because the faithful, who compose the Church, meet in it for prayer and Sacraments" (*The Longer Catechism of the Eastern Church*, questions 320–21).

Lutheran: "That we may obtain this faith, the Ministry of Teaching the Gospel and administering the Sacraments was instituted. . . . The Church is the congregation of saints, in which the Gospel is rightly taught and the Sacraments are rightly administered" (*Augsburg Confession*, articles V.1 and VII.1).

Reformed: "This catholic Church hath been sometimes more, sometimes less visible. And particular churches, which are members thereof, are more or less pure, according as the doctrine of the gospel is taught and embraced, ordinances administered, and public worship performed more or less purely in them" (*Westminster Confession of Faith*, chapter 25.4).

Anabaptist: "We believe in, and confess a visible church of God, namely, those who, as has been said before, truly repent and believe, and are rightly baptized; . . . this church, we say, may be known by their Scriptural faith, doctrine, love, and godly conversation, as, also, by the fruitful observance, practice, and maintenance of the true ordinances of Christ, which He so highly enjoined upon His disciples" (*Dordrecht Confession*, article 8).

Roman Catholic: "The sacred and holy, oecumenical and general Synod of Trent—lawfully assembled in the Holy Ghost, the same Legates of the Apostolic See presiding therein—to the end that the ancient, complete, and in every part perfect faith and doctrine touching the great mystery of the Eucharist may be retained in the holy Catholic Church. . . . The Catholic Church instituted, many years ago, the sacred Canon, so pure from every error. . . . For it is composed, out of the very words of the Lord, the traditions of the apostles, and the pious institutions also of holy pontiffs"

(*Canons and Decrees of the Council of Trent*, Session 22, Doctrine of the Sacrifice of the Mass).

Baptist: "We believe that a visible Church of Christ is a congregation of baptized believers, associated by covenant in the faith and fellowship of the gospel; observing the ordinances of Christ; governed by his laws, and exercising the gifts, rights, and privileges invested in them by his Word; that its only scriptural officers are Bishops, or Pastors, and Deacons, whose qualifications, claims, and duties are defined in the Epistles of Timothy and Titus" (*New Hampshire Baptist Confession*, article 13).

Wesleyan: "The visible Church of Christ is a congregation of faithful men, in which the pure Word of God is preached, and the sacraments duly administered, according to Christ's ordinance, in all those things that of necessity are requisite to the same" (*Methodist Articles of Religion*, article 13).

Liberal: "We can no longer think of the [worship] service as something demanded by God to which the worshiper is therefore compelled to submit. We must think of it as an exercise designed entirely to help the worshiper in securing the right religious attitude toward God, life, and duty. We must consider, then, the presuppositions with which our worshiper enters the church. The psychology of apperception is important here. We must estimate his attitude toward each element of worship. We must consider what may check the rising tide of emotion and what may carry it on to the full" (Gerald Birney Smith in *A Guide to the Study of the Christian Religion*, p. 617).

Point to Remember

God is spirit, and His worshipers must worship in spirit and in truth. John 4:24

To prepare for "The Way of the Church," read 1 Corinthians 12:12–31.

The Way of the Church

Is it then the walls that make Christians?

Victorinus, in *The Confessions of St. Augustine*

As an elder in his church, Nathan stopped to visit one of his fellow members who hadn't come to worship in several months. "We've missed you, Harold. Is anything wrong? Can we help you with anything?" "No, Nathan, nothing's really wrong. I've just been busy. A lot of important business demanded my attention, and I haven't had much time for church. But it's made me wonder, Nathan, do we really need to go to church? I believe that God is everywhere. Can't God bless me here just as easily as He can at church?" Nathan sighed to himself. He'd heard these questions before. Saying a silent prayer, he began to share his faith with Harold.

29. Is Harold right? Can God bless us anywhere—even if we're not within the walls of the church?

30. If God is with us everywhere, and will bless us, why does He want us to worship together?

Connected by Christ

When Christians gather together for worship, we experience a number of relationships. We are connected to the people we join for worship. We are brought into the presence of God "with angels and archangels and with all the company of heaven" (Hebrews 12:22–24).

23

In our study today, we explore the nature of these relationships in worship.

31. Different Christian churches use various terms to refer to worship services. For Lutherans, a common term is "Divine Service." When you think about it, this term can seem vague. Who is serving whom in worship? Is worship the acts of humans serving God or is it God serving humans? Does God need our worship?

32. Look at this list of elements that are often present in Christian worship. Which ones show God serving or giving to humans? In which ones do humans respond to God by serving or giving back to Him?

a. Time to worship (see Exodus 20:8–11 and Acts 20:7)

b. Confession of sins (1 John 1:9)

c. Absolution (forgiveness) of sins (1 John 1:9)

d. Praise (Psalm 9:1–2, Psalm 100:4, Revelation 5:12)

e. The Word of God (2 Timothy 3:14–17)

f. Offerings (Psalm 116:12–14, 17–19)

g. Baptism (Acts 2:38, 1 Peter 3:21)

h. The Lord's Supper (1 Corinthians 11:23–26)

i. Prayer (Matthew 7:7–8)

j. Benediction (Numbers 6:24)

33. Analyzing all of these elements of worship, who is really the servant in worship?

34. Our relationship to God is part of worship. As we worship, however, He has also brought us together with other people. What motivation do you see for this corporate worship in 1 Corinthians 12:12–14?

35. What additional reason for worship together do you see in Hebrews 10:25?

36. In the Smalcald Articles, Martin Luther writes that God gives His Gospel to us in many ways including the Word, Baptism, the Sacrament of the Altar, through the Power of the Keys (Absolution), "and also through the mutual conversation and consolation of brethren." (III:4). What do you think he means by this? How is this a powerful argument for worshiping together?

Challenges and Blessings

37. In worship God gives His gifts to us, but we often describe worship as our work. Why do you think we are so eager to take the credit for worship?

38. Psalm 116:12 asks "How can I repay the LORD for all His goodness to me?" Can we really give God anything to thank Him for His mercy? Does He need us? Read Psalm 116:12–14 to see how the psalmist answers this question.

39. God calls us together to be His church. Since the church is made up of redeemed sinners, there will be both challenges and blessings when we come together to worship. Discuss these challenges and blessings. Is our corporate worship worth the effort?

The Body of Christ

40. Read the first three paragraphs of the introduction to *Lutheran Worship* on page 6. What is the "rhythm of our worship" described by the writer?

41. We all serve as parts of the body of Christ. Take another look at 1 Corinthians 12:4–13:13. List below the names of some people at church who serve in ways mentioned by this passage. Can you see yourself in this passage?

Comparisons

As you read the following comparison quotes or summaries, look for how the different churches talk about the work of the Holy Spirit, whether through the means of grace or within a person.

Eastern Orthodox: "Is the Holy Ghost communicated to men even now likewise? He is communicated to all true Christians. . . . How may we be made partakers of the Holy Ghost? Through fervent prayer, and through the Sacraments" (*Longer Catechism of the Eastern Church*, questions 249–250).

Lutheran: "I believe that I cannot by my own reason or strength believe in Jesus Christ, my Lord, or come to Him; but the Holy Spirit has called me by the Gospel, enlightened me with His gifts, sanctified and kept me in the true faith" (Luther's Small Catechism, "The Creed," art. III). Lutherans emphasize that the Holy Spirit works through the means of grace: the Word and Sacraments.

Reformed: "But when God accomplishes His good pleasure in the elect, or works in them true conversion, He not only causes the gospel to be externally preached to them, and powerfully illuminates their minds by His Holy Spirit . . . but by the efficacy of the same regenerating Spirit He pervades the inmost recesses of the man" (*Canons of the Synod of Dort*, Art. XI).

Roman Catholic: The Holy Spirit awakens faith in unbelievers and communicates new life to them through the ministry of the church.

Anabaptist: This movement emphasizes the mystical work of the Spirit in the heart rather than through Word and Sacraments. Only holy people have received the Holy Spirit and are members of the church.

Baptist: "We believe that Repentance and Faith are sacred duties, and also inseparable graces, wrought in our souls by the regenerating Spirit of God" (*New Hampshire Baptist Confession*).

Wesleyan: "But as soon as he is born of God . . . he is now capable of hearing the inward voice of God, saying, 'Be of good cheer; thy sins are forgiven thee'; 'Go and sin no more.' . . . He 'feels in his heart,' to use the language of our Church, 'the mighty working of the Spirit of God'" (*Standard Sermons of John Wesley*, XXXIX.4).

Point to Remember

The body is a unit, though it is made up of many parts; and though all its parts are many, they form one body. So it is with Christ. For we were all baptized by one Spirit into one body—whether Jews or Greeks, slave or free—and we were all given the one Spirit to drink. 1 Corinthians 12:12–13

To prepare for "Elements of Christian Worship," skim Exodus 25–31.

Elements of Christian Worship

The standard of prayer is the standard of faith.

Attributed to Prosper of Aquitaine

Janet has been your friend since you were in high school. She has little background in Christianity, but always was curious about your faith. Recently, she has become a Christian and is looking for a church to join. "I'm confused," she says. "All of these churches say they are Christian, but they seem so different." "They all have a worship service, but they all do different things." "How can one religion have so many different expressions?"

42. Janet is correct in noticing differences in the way that different Christians worship. What differences have you noticed?

43. Where do you think these differences in worship come from?

In our last session we examined elements that are commonly used in Lutheran worship in order to ask the question, "Who is serving whom?" In this session we return to the content of worship to ask different questions. What elements are necessary in the Divine Service? What elements are helpful? How are these things manifest in the church's worship?

The Bible and Worship

44. When we look in the Bible, we might be surprised by what we find about worship. The Old Testament gives very specific directions on how to worship. Quickly browse through Exodus 25–31. What are

some of the features of worship found here? Are these still expected of Christians?

45. In contrast, the New Testament provides no detailed list of instructions on how Christians must worship. Yet it does provide descriptions of some early Christian worship, and some guiding principles for our worship. One of the first descriptions of worship after Pentecost is found in Acts 2:42. This verse contains four elements of Christian worship. What is the first one? (See also 1 Thessalonians 2:13) How does this find expression in our worship today? Why is this a vital element of Christian worship?

46. What is the second element of worship in the early church that is found in Acts 2:42? What does this mean? Why is this a significant element of Christian worship?

47. What is the third element of Christian worship found in Acts 2:42? What does this mean? (See also Luke 22:19 and 1 Corinthians 10:16.) Why is this an important element of Christian worship?

48. The Lutheran Confessions assume that the Lord's Supper will be celebrated regularly in Lutheran congregations. In fact, the confessions repeatedly claim that Lutheran congregations celebrate the Eucharist every Sunday. (See appendix p. 76.) Why do you think

Lutherans celebrate Holy Communion more often than some other churches?

49. What is the final element of worship found in Acts 2:42? How does this find expression in the worship and devotional life of Christians? What should be included when we do this? (See also 1 Timothy 2:1–2.)

50. Read James 5:16. What does this verse suggest we ought to do in worship and in our daily lives?

51. What common feature of worship do you see reflected in Hebrews 13:15 and Philippians 2:9–11? How is this present in our worship together?

52. Every element of worship we have examined can be enacted with spoken words alone. This is appropriate, but Scripture also indicates that another dimension may be used to amplify the Word. Read Ephesians 5:19–20. What do you see in this passage? How is this manifest in our worship?

Christian Freedom

53. Scripture doesn't give us these elements as a law. It never says "do these things or you are not a Christian." Why might Christians want to include these elements in their worship?

54. People often characterize worship by the label of the denomination. Are the elements of worship that we examined today "Lutheran"? Explain your answer.

55. In this session we have looked at general elements of worship. If these are present, do we still need to evaluate how they are used in a particular worship service? Explain your answer.

Explore the Scripture

56. The historic liturgy of the Christian church has all of the elements that we studied this week. Look closely at a setting of the Divine Service. Many parts of the liturgy come directly from Scripture. List below the passages you can easily find in the Bible.

57. What are some of your favorite hymns and songs? Why are they your favorite? Spend some time thinking about the words of these hymns and songs and how they reflect the truth of Scripture.

Comparisons

The form and content of Jewish worship in the first century greatly influenced the form and content of early Christian services (pp. 74–75). Below are some elements of worship that Jewish people are known to have used at the synagogue and at home during the first century. Note how they compare with some elements of the traditional Lutheran Divine Service.

Synagogue Service	Service of the Word
Readings from Torah and the Prophets	Reading from the Old Testament
Sermon	Sermon
Shema Israel Confession	Apostles' or Nicene Creed
Eighteen Benedictions	Congregational Prayers

Seder Service	Service of the Sacrament
The Kaddish Prayer	The Lord's Prayer
Cups of Wine	Cup of the Lord's Supper
Matzah Bread	Bread of the Lord's Supper
Narration of the Exodus	Narration of the Words of Institution
Singing of Hallel (Psalms 113–118	Post Communion canticle and hymns

A popular Aramaic prayer used in ancient Judaism is known as the Kaddish ("consecration"). Portions of this prayer are almost word for word the same as the Lord's Prayer, taught by Jesus. Note how the prayers are similar (italic text) and how they differ (regular text).

The Kaddish	The Lord's Prayer
Extolled and *hallowed be the name of God* throughout the world which He has created, and which He governs according to His righteous will. Just is He in all His ways and wise are all His decrees. *May His kingdom come,* and *His will be done in all the earth.* Praised be the Lord of life, the righteous Judge forever more. Whatsoever praise we would render unto God, howsoever we would adore the Most High, we would yet fail to give Him the glory due to His great name.	Our Father who art in heaven, *hallowed be thy name,* *thy kingdom come,* *thy will be done on earth* as it is in heaven. Give us this day our daily bread; and forgive us our trespasses as we forgive those who trespass against us; and lead us not into temptation but deliver us from evil.

Point to Remember

I will dwell among the Israelites and be their God. They will know that I am the LORD their God, who brought them out of Egypt so that I might dwell among them. I am the LORD their God. Exodus 29:45–46

To prepare for "When Scripture Is Silent," read Romans 14:13–23.

When Scripture Is Silent

For to those who believe in Christ whatever things are either enjoined or forbidden in the way of external ceremonies and bodily righteousnesses are all pure, adiaphora, and are permissible, except insofar as the believers are willing to subject themselves to these things of their own accord or for the sake of love.

Martin Luther, *Commentary on Galatians*

Holy Cross Lutheran Church was at a turning point. They had outgrown their building and had to do something. Should they seek a way to expand their sanctuary or should they build a new one? The congregation was divided. They decided that they would search the Scriptures to see what God wanted them to do. Both sides tried to quote Bible verses to support their position, but observers were quick to note that the verses really didn't fit this situation. They finally came to the conclusion that no Bible verse would give them a direct answer. (These situations are known as *adiaphora*, see glossary, p. 79.) Now what should they do?

58. How many questions do churches face that aren't directly addressed by Scripture? Give some examples.

59. Do Christians ever try to make Scripture answer questions that it doesn't address? Why is this a dangerous thing?

60. Do Christians ever ignore the counsel of God's Word when making decisions? Why is this dangerous?

God's Will

61. Read 2 Timothy 3:15–17. How are Christians to determine the will of God? What should we do when we learn His will? (See also Matthew 15:8–9.)

62. Are we bound to follow everything found in Scripture? See Romans 8:1–4 and Galatians 5:1.

63. When God's Word is silent about an issue (that is, it neither commands nor forbids us to do something), what is the Christian to do? See Romans 14:13–23.

64. When addressing issues on which Scripture is silent, we are bound to encounter differences of opinion. Look again at Romans 14:13–23. How are we to deal with those who are not convinced that a certain behavior is legitimate? See also 1 Corinthians 8:9.

65. Christians need to take care that they not become a stumbling block to the weak in faith. There is another danger in adiaphora, however. Those who are not truly weak in faith may try to bind other Christians to their own practice, and so rob them of the freedom of the Gospel. St. Paul encountered this situation regarding the issue of circumcision. Some Christians were insisting that all Christian men be circumcised even though the Bible does not require this. How does Paul respond in Galatians 2:3–5 and Galatians 5:1?

Note: The Lutheran Confessions deal extensively with the question of adiaphora. (See AC 14; Ap 14, and FC X.) Consider what the Epitome of the Formula of Concord says (pp. 77–78).

66. Other application of adiaphora may be seen in cases where no one seems to be in a position of taking offense. What counsel does 1 Corinthians 14:40 give for worship?

67. Another danger of adiaphora is that we begin to think that our human rites or customs, are good works that earn us something before God. Read 1 Timothy 4:1–5. What does this passage call the restriction of Christian freedom? What does Ephesians 2:8 tell us about relying on human works?

The Bible and Tradition

68. Issues of adiaphora, and therefore tensions, often arise as we are considering the traditions of a church. At times like this, we might be prone to point out that another person's viewpoint is just tradition, so we can get rid of it. How many useful or cherished things that you do are part of the traditions of your church? What are the benefits of these traditions? Are there any dangers to their observance?

69. The topic of adiaphora may make us uncomfortable. Two extreme reactions to these issues lead to problems. Legalism seeks to find a rule for everything. If Scripture doesn't speak, legalism fills in the blanks with regulations. The other extreme is antinomianism—a

rejection of God's Law, and an irresponsible, chaotic use of freedom. How do both of these fall short of God's plan? Are you ever tempted to fall into either of these abuses?

70. Freedom in adiaphora means that we do not all have to do things the same way. An individual congregation may choose to do a variety of things (on which Scripture is silent) that are different from other congregations. There may be significant advantages to be found, however, when churches choose to work together. What advantages might come from Christians voluntarily conforming to human standards?

Traditions and You

71. Spend some time thinking about the traditions that are part of your own Christian life. What has been the most meaningful or helpful? Is there anything that you would reconsider in the light of God's Word?

72. While these principles on dealing with adiaphora seem simple, they can be a challenge to apply. Consider your Christian freedom. Rejoice that Christ frees you from the Law's demands. How can you use your freedom in a way that is edifying and helpful to you and to other people?

Comparisons

Eastern Orthodox: "What is meant by the name *holy tradition*? By the name holy tradition is meant the doctrine of the faith, the law of God, the sacraments, and the ritual as handed down by the true believers and worshipers of God by word and example from one to another, and from generation to generation. . . . Why is tradition necessary even now? As a guide to the right understanding of holy Scripture, for the right ministration of the sacraments, and the preservation of sacred rites and ceremonies in purity of their original institution" (*The Longer Catechism of the Eastern Church*, questions 320–21).

Lutheran: "We believe, teach, and confess that the congregation of God of every place and every time has the power, according to its circumstances, to change such ceremonies in such manner as may be most useful and edifying to the congregation of God. Nevertheless, that herein all frivolity and offense should be avoided, and especial care should be taken to exercise forbearance towards the weak in faith" (*Formula of Concord, Epitome*, article X.4–5).

Reformed: "The greater the heap of ceremonies in the Church, so much the more is taken, not only from Christian liberty, but also from Christ, and from faith in Him; while the people seek those things in ceremonies which they should seek in the only Son of God, Jesus Christ, through faith. Wherefore a few moderate and simple rites, that are not contrary to the Word of God, do suffice the godly" (*Second Helvitic Confession*, chapter 27).

Anabaptist: The Anabaptists rejected all earlier liturgies. They emphasized weekly gatherings where people would seek the will of God and encourage one another to greater discipleship. They also taught that if Scripture did not command a practice, it probably should not be done by a Christian. As a result many Anabaptist groups have refused to use or own modern technology (cars, electricity, etc.) since Scripture does not mention these things.

Roman Catholic: An extensive tradition of canon law regulates the duties and practices of Roman Catholicism. At the heart of their worship is the canon of the mass.

Baptist: "In cases of difficulties or differences, either in point of doctrine or administration . . . it is according to the mind of Christ that many churches, holding communion together, do by their messengers meet to consider and give their advice in or about that matter in difference, to be reported to all the churches concerned; howbeit these messengers assembled are not intrusted with any church power properly so called, or with any jurisdiction over the churches themselves, to exercise any censures either over any churches or persons, to impose their determination of the churches or officers" (*Baptist Confession of 1688*, para. 15).

Wesleyan: "It is not necessary that rites and ceremonies should in all places be the same, or exactly alike; for they have been always different, and may be changed according to the diversity of countries, times, and men's manners, so that nothing be ordained against God's Word. Whosoever, through private judgment, willingly and purposely doth openly break the rites and ceremonies of the Church to which he belongs, which are not repugnant to the Word of God, and are ordained and approved by common authority, ought to be rebuked openly" (*Methodist Articles of Religion*, article 22).

Point to Remember

Let us therefore make every effort to do what leads to peace and to mutual edification. Romans 14:19

To prepare for "The Bible in Worship," read Isaiah 6:1–7.

The Bible in Worship

Lord, open now my heart to hear, And through Your Word
to me draw near; Preserve that Word in purity
That I Your child and heir may be.

Johannes Olearius

"Do I have to?" pleaded Andy. Theresa did not give in to her son. "Your grandparents sent you a wonderful present for your birthday. It is polite to thank them for their gift, and since you like it so much, to tell them." "I know," he replied, "but I don't know what to say." "I'll help you with the words," she said. "Let's work on it together." Andy sat down to write a thank-you note.

73. Have you ever struggled to find the right words for a letter or a thank-you note? Why?

74. Do you remember any times when your parents taught you how to do something that you thought was difficult (or a time when you taught your children)? How did they help you? How did it feel when you succeeded?

75. Do we need to *learn* how to worship? Explain your answer.

Growing through Worship

How do Christians learn to worship? For many, our education occurs simply through the Divine Services that we have attended. We learn about worship by worshiping with God's people. While there are different ways that Christians worship, many Christians have found it helpful to use scriptural verses and passages as the backbone of the Divine Service. God gives us His Word, and we respond to Him with His Word. We are not obligated to worship in this way, but we may find a great blessing through such richly biblical forms. In our study today, we will look up a number of passages from Holy Scripture. Hopefully, you will recognize these from your own use of them in the Divine Service.

76. Read Matthew 28:18–20. What part of our worship do we find here? What does this remind you about?

77. What words of worship reflect Matthew 15:22 and Mark 10:47?

78. The "Hymn of Praise" is another portion of the Divine Service. We sing many songs of praise at different times, but several texts find particular use in our worship. What do you hear in Luke 2:14? Whose words are these? Also look at Revelation 5:8–14. When do we sing these words? From whom do we get them?

79. Read John 6:68. At what point in the service do we sing these words? Why are these words of St. Peter particularly appropriate at that time?

80. There are several texts that are used as offertory songs. Read Psalm 51:10–12. What do we ask God as we sing these words? How does this help us keep our offerings in proper perspective?

81. While these are common texts in worship, not all are in use in all congregations. One of the most universally used passages of Scripture is Matthew 6:9–13. Is it necessary that we use these verses in worship? Why are these words so common?

82. As we prepare for Holy Communion, we know that we are about to enter the presence of Almighty God. Without His mercy we would not survive this encounter, but God does deal graciously with us. Read Isaiah 6:3–6 and Matthew 21:9. How are these words particularly appropriate in this context?

83. After the words of institution have been said, we sing a song asking Christ, the Lamb of God, for His mercy and peace. Read John 1:29 and Colossians 1:20. How does this title apply to Jesus Christ?

84. Several different songs of thanksgiving are sung after we have received the Blessed Sacrament. One of the oldest is found in Luke 2:29–32. When were these words first said? How do these words reflect our response to communion?

From the Heart

85. We have looked at some of the biblical texts reflected in our worship. There are many more in the Divine Service and in other orders of worship. There are also many biblical quotations, references, and allusions in our hymns and songs. Think about those worship texts that you know. When you learned these words, you were learning Scripture. How is this knowledge of Scripture an advantage for our Christian lives? (See Colossians 3:16.)

86. The liturgical texts that we have looked at are all part of "the ordinary." These are words that are repeated week after week in the Divine Service. Does this mean that worship will always be the same? How can we avoid falling into thoughtless repetition of words?

87. It is fairly common for Lutherans to describe these elements as "Lutheran worship." We have now seen that the texts are biblical texts. Have you ever seen or heard of these texts being used in non-Lutheran circles? What does this demonstrate about the Christian church?

Digging Deeper

88. We've looked at a number of worship texts and the scriptural references behind them, but we've only scratched the surface. Many other liturgical elements as well as many hymns and songs also reflect biblical texts. Discuss other references and allusions you discover.

89. The book of Revelation contains a number of references to worship in the life to come. Read some of these glorious descriptions in Revelation 4, 5, 7:9–17; and 19:4–10. What encouragement do they offer you?

There are a number of books on worship that you might find helpful in your continuing study. Consider one of the following, or ask your pastor for other suggestions:

Timothy Maschke, *Gathered Guests: A Guide to Lutheran Worship*. St. Louis: Concordia Publishing House, 2003.

James Leonard Brauer, *Meaningful Worship: A Guide to the Lutheran Service*. St. Louis: Concordia Publishing House, 1994.

Fred L. Precht, ed. *Lutheran Worship: History and Practice*. St. Louis: Concordia Publishing House, 1993.

Comparisons

Use of the Lord's Prayer as a Model: Anabaptists, Baptists, and some Wesleyans emphasize that Jesus gave the Lord's Prayer as a model and not as a form of prayer for repetition. They encourage spontaneous prayers from the heart rather than repeated prayers.

Formal Use of the Lord's Prayer: Most other Christians pray the Lord's Prayer daily or frequently in public worship. The official catechisms of the Eastern Orthodox, Lutheran, Reformed, and Roman Catholic churches contain commentaries on the Lord's Prayer. Repetition is only a problem if people repeat the words without considering what they say. Jesus Himself repeated prayers (Matthew 26:44).

Prayer with Non-Christians: Today, some Christians hold public prayer services with people of other religions. Interreligious services are most popular among Christians who have questioned traditional beliefs about the triune nature of God and do not consider joint services with non-Christians a threat to the Gospel. (In 1964 the Papal decree *Lumen Gentium* taught that Christians, Jews, and Muslims all pray to the same Creator.)

Point to Remember

Holy, holy, holy is the LORD Almighty; the whole earth is full of His glory. Isaiah 6:3

Leader Guide

This guide is provided as a "safety net," a place to turn for help in answering questions and for enriching discussion. It will not answer every question raised in your class. Please read it, along with the questions, before class. Consult it in class only after exploring the Bible references and discussing what they teach. Please note the different abilities of your class members. Some will easily find the Bible passages listed in this study; others will struggle. To make participation easier, team up members of the class. For example, if a question asks you to look up several passages, assign one passage to one group, the second to another, and so on. Divide the work! Let participants present the answers they discover.

Each topic is divided into four easy-to-use sections.

Focus: introduces key concepts that will be discovered.

Inform: guides the participants into Scripture to uncover truths concerning a doctrine.

Connect: enables participants to apply what is learned in Scripture to their lives and provides them an opportunity to formulate and articulate a defense of a key doctrine.

Vision: provides participants with practical suggestions for extending the theme of the lesson out of the classroom and into the world.

Also take note of the Comparisons section at the end of each lesson. The editor has drawn this material from the official confessional documents and historical works of the various denominations. The passages describe and compare the denominations so that students can see how Lutherans differ from other Christians and also see how all Christians share many of the same beliefs and practices. The passages are not polemical.

The God We Worship

Objectives

By the power of the Holy Spirit working through God's Word, we will (1) see that only the triune God is worthy of our worship and praise, (2) believe that we have access to God because we have been redeemed by Jesus Christ, and (3) respond to God's gracious gifts in worship.

Opening Worship

Sing together "Come, O Almighty King" (*LW* 169).

Focus

Ask a volunteer to read the introductory paragraph, then discuss the questions.

1. Answers will vary. Remind participants that our first reactions may fall short of what they should be. It is easy to get caught up in discussing the details of worship, or the controversies that often surround it, while forgetting the true focus of our worship. While allowing participants to discuss their first reactions, keep the conversation focused. Many issues will be discussed in this study. This is only the first introduction.

2. Allow participants the opportunity to briefly evaluate the focus of worship.

Why Worship? (Inform)

3. God is worthy of worship. His glory, splendor, holiness, and greatness are so wonderful that all creatures should be moved to worship Him. Every good thing, all that we are and have comes from Him. He deserves our worship because He is God.

4. Exodus 20:8 reveals the third commandment to us. God commands His people to worship Him. Hebrews 10:25 reminds us that worship does not end with the coming of Christ. Christians are also

48

called to continue to worship together—in part to give each other encouragement in the last days.

5. Luther reminds us that the purpose of the Sabbath was not simply to have a day off from work, but to provide opportunity to worship. He directed people's attention to the Word of God. We hear God's voice, and receive His direction through His Word. True worship must involve the proclamation and belief of God's Holy Word. God knows that we will be blessed as we hear His Word.

6. A god is whatever we trust and believe in. Whatever being or thing that we trust above all other things is, in fact, our god. To be sure, there is only one true, living God. Only the true God can save us. Only He has the power that we need. Only He is truly worthy of worship. Yet many people continue to worship false gods. Understood in this way, every person has a god.

7. Deuteronomy 6:4 reminds us that there is only one God. Matthew 28:19 reveals that this one God consists of three persons: Father, Son, and Holy Spirit. The biblical doctrine of the Trinity is beyond our human comprehension. Our limited brains are incapable of fully understanding the nature of God. We can, however, trust and believe His Word. The only true God is the Holy Trinity. The three persons, Father, Son, and Holy Spirit, are each fully God, and yet are only one God. This is how God has revealed Himself to us.

8. Jesus, who is the way, the truth, and the life, says that it is impossible to access the Father apart from the Son. Without the Son, we do not really know the Father. 1 Corinthians 12:3 teaches us that we cannot believe in Jesus without the Holy Spirit. We are not free to ignore the Trinity or any of the three persons. We come to the Father through Jesus. We believe in Jesus through the Spirit. The Trinity is the only true God. This is the God we worship.

9. In Isaiah 42, God forbids worshiping false gods, or any created thing. In Revelation 22, St. John was about to worship an angel who had shown him wondrous things. The angel rebuked him. Angels are not worthy of worship—they are servants of God along with human beings. (This shows us also that mere human beings are not worthy of worship either.) Only God is worthy of worship.

True Worship (Connect)

10. We have seen that God is worthy of worship. He commands our worship, and invites us to worship Him by offering us His

blessings of forgiveness, life, and salvation. True worship must be focused on the true God. God has revealed Himself as the Holy Trinity. We have certainly engaged in false worship. We have let other things take the place of God. (Indeed, every sin we commit is also a sin against the first commandment. When we sin, we show that we prefer sin to God.) Since we have done these things, we should do as God says: confess our sins and receive His forgiveness for Jesus' sake.

11. Worship and faith are directly related. Worship reflects our faith and the content of our faith is affected by the way we worship. God's revelation of Himself moves us to worship Him as He is. Our faith and doctrine were never meant to be merely thoughts or words. Our faith impacts every aspect of our lives—including worship.

12. Answers will vary. We worship God because of who He is, in thanksgiving for the salvation that is ours in Jesus Christ, in praise of His goodness to us, and because He gives us His gifts in worship. Allow participants the time to discuss things that move them to respond to God in worship.

One Triune God (Vision)

13. Each of these commands is about worship. They appear at the beginning of the Ten Commandments because our relationship with God has the highest priority. In Matthew 22:37, Jesus summarizes these commands with one word: "love."

14. Answers may vary. Common expressions such as "Glory be to the Father, and to the Son, and to the Holy Spirit" focus our worship on the Holy Trinity.

15. Answers will vary. Encourage participants to pick out someone they could invite and keep in their prayers this week.

The People Who Worship

Objectives

By the power of the Holy Spirit working through God's Word, we will (1) see that we need God's gift of faith in order to truly worship Him, (2) recognize that worship must conform to the truth of God's Word, and (3) apply our faith in worship and in every aspect of our lives.

Opening Worship

Recite Psalm 51:1–13.

Focus

Ask a participant to read the introductory paragraph, then briefly discuss the questions.

16. There may be a number of responses to the son's complaint. His words seem to indicate he's uncomfortable with his mother's question. Perhaps he is masking his guilt at being unable to answer her. Maybe he did not want to attend worship. We may be tempted to lash out at words like these, but chances are we can relate to them at times. Be sure to emphasize that it is not enough to simply "go to church." If we are not hearing the Word of God and thereby receiving His blessings, we are not really worshiping Him.

17. Be careful that responses to this question do not turn into a criticism of other people. The question is about each individual. There may be times that we treat worship more as a "spectator sport" than something that we are called to participate in gladly and freely. We may do this because it is easier just to attend a service than to take part in it. We may participate less if we are not familiar with the worship forms or with what is expected of us. There may be times when we seem less able to take part in a service. We need to be careful that we do not use times like these as an excuse. Worship is not a magical

formula or ritual that we simply witness. It calls for the involvement of each Christian.

In Spirit and Truth (Inform)

18. The Samaritan woman tries to sidetrack Jesus by bringing up a point of controversy between the Jews and the Samaritans—the proper place for worship. She wants to know where people have to worship. Does it have to be in Jerusalem as the Jews teach, or is she free to worship in other places? Jesus does not mandate any city as the one place of worship. Instead, He teaches that true worshipers worship "in spirit and in truth." It is true that God once taught that worship should take place in the temple in Jerusalem. Now that God had become incarnate in Jesus Christ, worship was not limited to this one place. It is not the place of worship that matters, but the God who is worshiped. The woman wanted to know where to worship. Jesus was teaching her how to worship. She needed to worship not by simply going to a place of worship, but by worshiping in spirit. The inclination of her heart was vital. To worship in spirit means to believe, to worship with your heart as well as your mind and body.

19. The Apology of the Augsburg Confession echoes Jesus' words by stressing the necessity of belief. Faith and worship are completely connected. Worship is not only something we do because we believe—our faith itself is worship. Trusting and believing God is worship. When we receive His gifts (and we only receive His spiritual gifts by faith), we are worshiping. This is part of God's plan for us. He is pleased when we believe Him and receive His gifts.

20. 1 John 1:8–9 and Psalm 32:5 (which are often used in worship) remind us that we are sinners in need of God's forgiveness. This is true even if we try to ignore this fact. Thankfully, God is gracious and merciful. He forgives our sins for Christ's sake. When we confess our sins, we are acknowledging what we bring to worship—our sinfulness. We are utterly reliant on God's grace if we are to come into His presence and receive His blessing. Faith knows that we owe everything to Christ, and it boldly reaches out to receive His blessings. Even when the service does not begin with Confession and Absolution, we come before God with repentant hearts each day of our lives, knowing that He forgives us in Jesus Christ. (See Apology, p. 76.)

21. It is not sufficient to do or say anything we want. God tells us to worship in truth. Our worship must be true—it is normed and guided

by the Word of God which is truth (John 17:17). This does not mean that everything we say must be a word-for-word quote from the Bible, but we judge our words and our worship by the standard of God's Holy Word. It is our only infallible guide.

As our guide, the Holy Scriptures direct us to proclaim the Truth made flesh, Jesus Christ. The apostle John uses the word *truth* in his Gospel to describe Jesus (John 1:14, 17; 14:6), Jesus' teachings (John 8:31–32, 45–46), and the Spirit's testimony about Jesus (14:7; 15:26; 16:13). Worshiping "in spirit and in truth" will not center on emotional experiences, seeking miracles, or so-called "spiritual" phenomena, but on the clear proclamation of the Gospel of Jesus Christ in Word and Sacrament. The Scriptures assure us that the Holy Spirit works powerfully through these means of grace (1 Peter 1:23; Titus 3:5; John 20:22–23; Matthew 26:27–28).

22. Hosea 6:6 (which Jesus quotes in Matthew 9:13 and Matthew 12:7) makes it clear that God was never asking simply for outward obedience. He has always sought the whole person. Repeatedly in the Old Testament, God calls Israel to offer sacrifices. When the sacrifices were offered without faith, God called His people to acknowledge Him and show mercy. Without these responses of faith, the sacrifices meant nothing. In the same way, Christians who have been freed from offering animal sacrifices are still called to trust and believe our God. Without faith in Christ, we are not worshiping.

23. Romans 12:1 calls us to offer ourselves, our bodies, as living sacrifices to God. We do this in response to God's goodness to us. He has freely shown us His mercy. We respond by gratefully offering ourselves to Him. This is not a sacrifice of blood and death. Christ has already offered the final sacrifice of His body on the cross. Instead, God calls us to offer ourselves as a living sacrifice. He calls us to serve Him with our bodies. When our lives reflect our faith, we are doing this. Yet even the opportunity and ability to do this are blessings from God. We would be unable to serve God unless He had first served us.

By Faith Alone (Connect)

24. Worship is never to be a mere outward performance of words or actions. Whatever forms or words we use to worship, we may be tempted to believe that the acts themselves are worship. We need to confess this attitude and receive God's forgiveness. He calls us to worship in spirit and truth.

25. Don't question the sincerity of people in other religions. People can be sincere but also wrong! No act of worship is of any use if it is not directed, in faith, to the true and living God, the Holy Trinity. Non-Christians are not engaged in true worship or belief. See appendix p. 77.

26. We must remember that God wants all people to believe in Him and receive His gift of salvation. Those who have received this gift respond in worship and thanksgiving. When we encounter people who do not worship the true God, we need to remember that Jesus Christ also died and rose for them. We should share the Gospel with them so that they may receive God's salvation and join us in worshiping Him.

Taking Stock (Vision)

27. We need God's forgiveness not only before services, but daily. Remember to take the time to confess your sins and hear His forgiveness each day.

28. Answers will vary. Encourage participants to try these suggestions in the coming week.

The Way of the Church

Objectives

By the power of the Holy Spirit working through God's Word, we will (1) examine the many ways that God serves us in worship, (2) respond to God's gracious gifts as we worship Him, and (3) recognize God's call to us to live as part of the body of Christ, the Church.

Opening Worship

Sing "Christ Is Our Cornerstone" (*LW* 290).

Focus

Ask a volunteer to read the introductory paragraph, then discuss the questions. Participants may know people like Harold and Nathan. We should be careful not to name names or get too specific about other people as we discuss these questions.

29. Harold has a point. God truly is omnipresent. He is not limited by our human restrictions. He can bless us anywhere. In fact, He does bless us. All good things that we receive in this life are from God. He blesses us even when we fail to recognize Him as the source of our blessings.

30. God can bless us anywhere, but He promises His blessings of forgiveness, life, and salvation in His Word and Sacraments. He promises that He is present where two or more Christians are gathered in Jesus' name. We worship together because this is God's plan for us. He has told us to do this, and has promised us great blessings when we worship together.

Connected by Christ (Inform)

31. This is a very important question, and helps illustrate some of the differences in how various denominations conceive of worship. Many Christians think worship is primarily something that we do for God. We praise Him. We give Him offerings. We serve Him. Yet as

we consider various elements of worship, we will see that many of them are occasions where He serves us. Christian worship may contain both aspects. God graciously gives to us, and we respond to Him in faith and thanksgiving. It is important that we recognize that God does not need our worship. There is nothing that God needs. He is God no matter how His creation responds to Him.

32. a. Time is part of God's gift to us. It is His creation. In Exodus 20, we hear the third commandment's call for us to worship, yet in that command is also the blessing of time. God gave His people a day of rest so that they would have the opportunity to worship Him. While Christians are not obligated to keep the Sabbath (Matthew 12:8, Colossians 2:16–17), Acts 20:7 shows us that they commonly met together on Sunday, "the Lord's Day." They met for worship on the day in which Christ rose from the dead, as well as at other times. It is true that we use some of "our" time for worship, but we should remember that the time itself was first a gift from God.

b. God provides us with the opportunity and invitation to confess our sins. We are sinners who need God's forgiveness. At His invitation, we acknowledge our sinful nature, and admit where we have disobeyed God's commands in thought, word, and deed.

c. Absolution (and the forgiveness of sins we hear in other parts of the service) is a gracious gift of God. Nothing we do earns or merits this treatment. He has given to us what we did not deserve— forgiveness and life in Jesus Christ.

d. These verses are just a few examples of the many passages that call for God's people to praise Him. We praise God as we respond to His gifts, acknowledge His identity and goodness to us, as we proclaim His greatness, and we sing and rejoice in Him. Revelation 5:12 reminds us that we praise Him because He is worthy of all praise and glory.

e. While it is people who read the Word, the Word itself comes from God. All Scripture is inspired by God. He has given us His Word so that we may know His will and come to faith in His Son. We do not need to guess what God desires or what He might say. He freely communicates to us in the Bible. The Word is one of His gifts to us.

f. Our offerings are clearly examples of us giving to God. We give financial offerings, but also offer ourselves and our time. We support the mission and ministry of His Church in our offerings.

However, even here we are not taking the initiative. God has first given us all things. We only give back a portion of what He has given to us.

g. In Baptism, God gives His blessings to His people. He gives forgiveness of sins and salvation through this blessed washing. We do nothing to deserve these blessings, but He still gives them to us. While we only undergo Baptism once, we continue to live in its blessings each day. In fact, the words that begin most worship services are meant to remind us of Baptism: "In the name of the Father and of the Son and of the Holy Spirit." Each service begins with a reminder that we worship as the baptized and forgiven children of God.

h. In the Lord's Supper, Christ our risen Lord is the host who invites us to eat His true body and drink His true blood once offered in sacrifice on the cross. He gives us life and forgiveness again. He gives Himself to us.

i. As we pray, we bring our concerns, requests, and supplications before God. We do this, however, at His invitation and with His help. He tells us to ask Him for His help, because He wants to help, even as a father wants to help his children. Luther's Small Catechism summarizes this well in its explanation to the introduction of the Lord's Prayer: "God tenderly invites us to believe that He is our true Father and that we are His true children, so that with all boldness and confidence we may ask Him as dear children ask their dear father."

j. A benediction is a blessing (literally, a "good word.") God blesses us and sends us forth in His peace. This is also His work.

33. While we are indeed responding to God's gifts, He gives far more than we could ever give. All that we do is return a tiny portion of what He has first given to us. God graciously serves us in worship.

34. 1 Corinthians 12:12–14 (and the verses that follow) compare the church to a body. God has brought us together to be one body in Christ. Christ is the head of the body, and each of us is a part of this collective body. The word *member* refers to a part of a body (such as a limb). The idea of church membership is rooted in this understanding and should not be compared with participation in a club. We worship together because God has placed us together in one body. He has given us different gifts and abilities so that together, living under Him, we can accomplish more things than we could do separately. The church, and corporate worship are His idea. We need each other.

35. Hebrews 10:25 reminds us that as we worship together we are able to encourage one another. We cannot do this if we are not with other Christians.

36. Luther supports these words with Matthew 18:20 "For where two or three come together in my name, there I am with them." God blesses us as Christians fellowship together, share God's Word and counsel with each other, and support one another in the Christian faith. These are functions of the church that we simply cannot do alone. We need each other. I can be a Christian by myself, but I cannot be the church by myself.

Challenges and Blessings (Connect)

37. Answers will vary. It is common for Christians to put more of themselves into this than we ought. It does feel like we are the ones acting at times, but still we know that God gives us the means and the ability to do these things. It may be that we want to be in control. We want to feel useful and needed. In much of our spiritual life, we may struggle with wanting a greater role for ourselves than we really have. Yet God still loves us and blesses us for Jesus sake. Even when we make too much of ourselves, He blesses us.

38. In a very real sense, there is nothing we can do to repay God. We might give Him offerings, but these are only a return of things He has given us first. He graciously receives our gifts and our worship not because of the intrinsic value of these things, but because He loves us. A parent, who receives an otherwise ugly and useless gift, loves the gift if it was given to them in love by their child. So our Father graciously receives our worship because He loves us. He loves us because of who we are in Jesus. So the Psalmist answers, how can I repay God? By receiving His salvation and responding in worship.

39. Be careful to keep this discussion positive, and not degenerate into a gripe session against other church members. There are challenges when sinners worship together. Not all members will likely see things the same way. There will be different preferences for style, music, time, and many other aspects of worship. Some of these have a scriptural basis, others may not. Whatever the challenges may be, God has called us to be a church. The blessings of our relationship far outweigh the challenges. God intends to bless us as we live together in the body of Christ. He knows how much we need one another.

The Body of Christ (Vision)

40. We speak back to God what He has first spoken to us through the Scripture.

41. Answers will vary.

Elements of Christian Worship

Objectives

By the power of the Holy Spirit working through God's Word, we will (1) rejoice that Christ has freed us from the Law by His death and resurrection, (2) search the Scriptures to see the basic components of worship in the early Christian church, and (3) see the application of biblical texts and teachings in worship.

Opening Worship

Recite the Apostles' Creed.

Focus

42. The introduction starts to address some of our biggest questions about worship—the different ways that Christians worship. In this session we will be talking about the fundamental elements of worship. Allow participants a few minutes to discuss things that they have seen. Some of the major differences include the type of music that is used, the role of the pastor and other leaders, the presence of vestments or other special clothing, the "formality" or "informality" of the service, the degree of involvement by the congregation, and the use (or non-use) of the Sacraments.

43. This may be a difficult question. Many differences in worship reflect different theological understandings. For example, the use of the Lord's Supper will reflect what a church believes about this Sacrament. Some may come from the cultural background of the church and its worshipers. Some differences reflect different views of the purpose of worship. Some may be questions of style or preference. These are only a few of the sources of the differences.

The Bible and Worship (Inform)

44. Exodus 25–31 is one of the sections of Scripture that gives specific directions for worship in the Old Testament. In Exodus 25

God tells His people how to construct the Ark of the Covenant, the table for the bread of the presence and the lamp stand. In chapters 26–27, God gives the design for the tabernacle—the place where His glory would dwell and for the altar of burnt offerings—where the priests were to offer burnt offerings. Chapter 28 gives specific directions for the type of clothing that the priests would wear in worship. In chapter 29, the priests are consecrated and set apart for service in the tabernacle. Chapters 30 and 31 involve the production of various furnishings for the temple, and give instructions for their use. Chapter 31 also tells them about the Sabbath. This is an amazing amount of detail. God tells Israel exactly what they are to do in worship. We must note that these things are part of the old covenant and are no longer practiced by Christians. John 1:14 tells us that Christ, the Word, became flesh and *tabernacled* among us. In Christ, God is no longer limiting Himself to the tabernacle of the old covenant. The Book of Hebrews teaches us that Christ is the fulfillment of the priesthood and of sacrifice. We do not worship in this way now that Christ has come and has offered Himself as the final sacrifice.

45. The first thing that Acts 2:42 tells us is that the early Christians devoted themselves to the apostles' teaching. The content of the apostles' teaching is the Word of God, as 1 Thessalonians 2:13 reminds us. (Remember that Acts 2 records events at the very beginning of the Christian church. The New Testament has not yet been written by the apostles. As eyewitnesses to Jesus, they themselves were the source of information about Jesus.) As the early church listened to the apostles' teaching in worship, so we do also. The presence of God's Word is a vital element of Christian worship. Without the reading of Holy Scripture, we are not hearing the Word of God, but the word of men. Most Lutheran congregations, like many other Christian churches, choose to read the Scriptures from a schedule of readings called a *lectionary*. This schedule is designed to read a wide variety of Scripture in worship, and keeps us from reading only our favorite passages. It helps us to hear the whole counsel of God. The Word is also present as it is proclaimed and applied to our current situation by the sermon.

46. The second element of worship is fellowship (in Greek, *koinonia*). Fellowship is a very close relationship, a group of people who share things in common. Christians gather in fellowship when we have a common faith, share the same beliefs, and hold a set of

common, biblical values. Fellowship reminds us that we are called not only to be individual Christians but to be part of the church. This is still true today. While we will engage in a devotional life and private or individual worship of God, we are also called to fellowship with the people of God. We worship together, just as the early Christians did. So much did they value this fellowship that they continued to worship together even when the church was facing persecution and Christians were being killed for their faith.

47. The third element of worship reflected in Acts 2:42 is "the breaking of bread." While "breaking bread" can refer to any meal shared together (as in Acts 2:46), here, in the context of worship, it refers to Holy Communion. The early Christians were not only hearing the Word when they came to worship in fellowship, they were also communing together. We see this reflected in worship whenever the Lord's Supper is celebrated according to Christ's institution.

48. Lutherans have a frequent celebration of the Lord's Supper because of Christ's gracious invitation to do this, and because of its benefits. We believe that Christ is truly present in this Sacrament, in His body and blood, for our forgiveness. Seeing these wonderful gifts, and hearing God's invitation to commune, why wouldn't we want to celebrate the Supper often? In contrast, some churches that do not believe that Christ is really present, or who think that the bread and wine are mere symbols, tend to have communion less frequently.

49. The fourth element of worship referenced in Acts 2:42 is prayer. God has invited His children to come to Him in prayer at any time. Prayer should certainly be a part of our corporate worship, but it should also be part of our personal devotions and daily lives. We are exhorted to pray at all times and for all of our concerns and needs. 1 Timothy 2:1–2 shows us some of the things for which we ought to pray. We should offer requests, prayers, intercessions, and thanksgiving. We ask God for what we need and desire, we pray for others, and we thank God for His goodness. We pray for all people, especially for those who do not yet know the Savior. We pray for our government, and for peace. Our Father invites us to bring all of our needs and concerns to Him in prayer.

50. James 5:16 reminds us of the importance of Confession and Absolution. As we enter into the presence of our God, we do so dressed only in Christ's righteousness. We confess our sins and hear His forgiveness. While Confession and Absolution are not present in

every worship service, they are a part of our daily Christian lives. Even when there is not a specific order of Confession and Absolution, no Christian worship service is complete without a call to repentance and the proclamation of the forgiveness of sins.

51. Hebrews 13:15 enjoins us to offer God a sacrifice of praise. It specifies that we do this when we confess His name. Philippians 2 points to the great day when every knee will bow before Christ and every tongue will confess that He is Lord. When we worship we are confessing our faith. We acknowledge to one another and to the world that we believe in the true God. We proclaim to anyone who will listen that we know that Jesus Christ is the Savior of the world. We see this as we confess our faith together in the Creeds—summaries of our belief.

52. Ephesians 5:19–20 reminds us of the helpfulness of music. We make music in our heart to the Lord, but also speak to one another in hymns, songs, and spiritual songs. Music can be a beautiful and enriching aspect of worship.

Christian Freedom (Connect)

53. These are helpful elements of worship. The early Christians did these things because they found that they were important elements of worship. They joined together, heard God's Word, celebrated the Lord's Supper, and prayed. They sang songs, confessed their sins and their faith, and heard God's blessing. These were not a burden to them but a blessing. They knew that God was working in their lives through these things. So we also receive these elements of worship not as a burden but as a wonderful invitation. God allows and invites us to do these things.

54. There are some differences in how denominations understand particular elements (e.g., What is the Lord's Supper? Is the Bible really the Word of God?) Nonetheless, these elements are used, to some degree, in all Christian denominations. Even the historic liturgy is not specifically Lutheran. We share liturgical texts and structures, hymns and songs with other Christians. Our use of these elements will reflect our biblical doctrine, yet to the degree they are shared with other Christians, they testify to the true unity of the "one, holy, Christian and apostolic church."

55. Simply having Bible readings or prayers or any other element does not automatically make the worship appropriate or good. One can

read the Scriptures without reference to Christ and His salvation. That would not be Christian worship. Some people pray to other gods or for things which are rejected by the Bible. This would not be Christian worship. We need to evaluate our worship (and everything we do) in the light of God's Word.

Explore the Scripture (Vision)

56. Answers will vary.
57. Answers will vary.

When Scripture Is Silent

Objectives

By the power of the Holy Spirit working through God's Word, we will (1) know that, by Christ's death and resurrection, He has freed us from the Law's demands, (2) thankfully live in Christian freedom while being considerate of those who are weak in the faith, and (3) allow others to live in Christian freedom.

Opening Worship

Sing "O Word of God Incarnate" (*LW* 335)

Focus

Read the introductory paragraph, then briefly discuss the questions.

58. Many things that we face every day are not directly addressed by Scripture. The example in our introduction is one: should a church remodel or rebuild? Where should a church be built? What should it look like? What times should services be held? Which of our faithful and qualified Christians will teach a Sunday school class? The Bible may give us some principles to consider, but we cannot look in our concordances to see what color the church should be painted.

59. Unfortunately, Christians do try to do this at times. If Scripture really does speak to an issue, we must listen. But we must not take Scripture out of context or twist it to say things that are not really there. When we make it appear that Scripture says something that it really doesn't, we are taking the place of God. We are making our word more important than His Word. We also risk the faith of other people. If they reject our misuse of Scripture, they may also reject the proper use of Scripture. It is vitally important to read Scripture in context.

60. This error is just as dangerous as misapplying or twisting God's Word. When we ignore God's Word and fail to listen to it, we

have substituted our own reason for God's wisdom. We are blessed when we hear the Word of God and keep it (Luke 11:28).

God's Will (Inform)

61. Christians determine God's will by consulting His Word. It is the only infallible guide that we have. We carefully search the Scriptures to see if they address the topic that we are considering. If the Bible does speak to an issue, we are to listen to the Word. We are not free to ignore God's Word. He has the final say. When we ignore the Bible, we may end up in the situation Jesus warns about in Matthew 15:8–9: proclaiming human teachings instead of God's Word. When we do this, we worship Him in vain, having already rejected Him and His will.

62. All Scripture is inspired by God and is His Word. However, Christ Jesus has fulfilled the Law and freed us from its demands. We no longer offer animal sacrifices, for example, because Christ has offered the final sacrifice of Himself on the cross. We are not required to eat kosher foods or outwardly observe the Sabbath Day because Jesus has fulfilled these things for us. We no longer live under the Law, but by the Gospel. This does not mean, however, that we should go on sinning. Romans 6:15 makes it clear that we are not to use God's grace as an excuse for sinning. We are no longer slaves to sin, but we are servants of God.

63. Issues on which Scripture is truly silent are known as *adiaphora*. When you think about it, many things that we deal with every day are adiaphora. (Some of these were discussed in the introduction.) In cases where the Bible doesn't tell us to do something, and doesn't tell us not to do it, the Christian is free to act according to his own conscience and preference. Romans 14:13–23 uses the example of foods. Are Christians to follow Jewish dietary restrictions? Scripture does not require us to do this, nor does it forbid us to follow kosher guidelines. A Christian is free to eat kosher or non-kosher food. Paul gives two guiding principles. One is that whatever we do must come from faith. If we are doubting whether something is right, we shouldn't do it. But if we are confident that God does not forbid it, we are free to act as we see fit. The second guideline is addressed in the next question.

64. We need to be careful that we do not use our God-given freedom in a manner that causes a weaker Christian to stumble in the

faith. We are not to become stumbling blocks or obstacles to other Christians. This word is sometimes translated as "offense." An offense in this case does not mean something that another person doesn't like. It means something that can cause them to stumble or fall from the faith. We are indeed free to do many things, but we do not want to use our freedom in such a careless manner that we cause another person to fall from faith. This calls stronger Christians to be watchful for those who are weak. We may need to be careful in our use of freedom so that we do not harm the faith of a weaker brother or sister. The Lutheran Confessions emphasize the responsible use of freedom, saying that we should not give offense to the weak and cause them to grow hostile towards the Gospel. We also should not use our freedom frivolously and so cause others to take offense. (See appendix p. 77.)

65. In both references (and in the rest of Galatians), St. Paul strongly upholds Christian freedom. The Judaizers were insisting that people had to follow their own, non-biblical rules in order to be genuine Christians. This is not true, and is an offense to the Gospel. It places our human regulations above God's Word. Our observance of human rites does not make us Christians. In the face of such persecution, Paul did not allow Titus to undergo circumcision, and advised the Galatian church to likewise reject the demand for circumcision. It was not the outward act that was the problem, but the motive. The Judaizers would not be allowed to steal the freedom of the Gospel from others.

(It is interesting to note that in Acts 16:3, Paul was taking Timothy to evangelize practicing Jews. These Jews would genuinely have stumbled if they learned that Timothy was not circumcised. In this situation, Paul circumcised Timothy. For the sake of the weak, they were happy to concede. In Galatia, the Judaizers were not weak in faith. They were trying to control the lives of others, to make everyone like they were.)

66. 1 Corinthians 14:40 reminds us that when we worship together, we need to be concerned about how our actions affect others. Even if we have freedom to do certain things, we don't want worship to be chaotic or disorderly. We don't want to use our freedom in a way that is disruptive to the worship of others. Instead, everything done in worship should be done "in a fitting and orderly way."

67. 1 Timothy 4:1–5 calls the restriction of Christian freedom a demonic doctrine. If we are restricting people from doing what God

has freed them to do, we are not serving Him, but serving the devil. Ephesians 2:8 emphatically tells us that we are saved by God's grace, not by our own works. We dare not offer our own works and ideas as a substitute for the work of Christ. We are saved by His life, death, and resurrection alone.

The Bible and Tradition (Connect)

68. Keep this discussion focused on traditions that are received positively. It is far too easy to criticize the traditions of others without looking at our own. While many traditions will be obvious, others may be overlooked. Things like the date of Christmas, the time and day when worship services are held, wedding customs, and countless other aspects of our church life are not directly addressed in Scripture. These traditions help give us a group identity. They make it possible for us to worship together. They provide order and structure to the things that we do together. If we are not careful, however, our traditions can eclipse the Gospel. We can exclude others with our traditions. We can begin to assume that everything we do is found in Scripture. We should boldly and freely use the best of our human traditions, but acknowledge them for what they are.

69. Both of these positions compromise God's Word. Legalism strips away the freedom that Christ has won for us, and binds us to the Law again. It ultimately relies on works and our own efforts. As it binds consciences to human standards, it eclipses the Gospel and leads to despair. Antinomianism seeks freedom at any cost. It cares little for the effect it has on other people. It is self-serving, and creates stumbling blocks for other people. Both are abuses that fall short of God's plan. Sadly, we are inclined to both errors. We want freedom for ourselves while seeking to bind other people to our own preferences and understanding. We want to be legalistic for them and antinomian for ourselves.

70. Answers will vary. There are some significant advantages to conformity in adiaphora. When we work together, we may find it much easier to worship with other Christian congregations. Uniformity in our practice helps children learn and remember, and is a source of comfort for the elderly. (Think how hard it would be if we all used different versions of the Lord's Prayer!) Christians do not have to worship on Sunday, but the availability and prevalence of worship on Sunday mornings is a strong witness to our world. A considerate use of our

freedom may promote peace in the church. Allow participants the time to discuss other benefits of voluntary cooperation on adiaphora.

Traditions and You (Vision)

71. Answers will vary.
72. Answers will vary.

The Bible in Worship

Objectives

By the power of the Holy Spirit working through God's Word, we will (1) review the biblical foundation of the Divine Service, (2) recognize that the Lutheran Divine Service is an expression of the worship of the entire Christian church, and (3) be moved to respond to God's grace in Christ Jesus with worship and thanksgiving.

Opening Worship

Sing "Oh, that I Had a Thousand Voices" (*LW* 448).

Focus

73. This is a common experience. The more we care about the letter or about the people receiving it, the more we want the words to be just right. We don't want to say the wrong thing, and we want to be sure we communicate accurately.

74. It can be hard to learn new and challenging things, but this is part of our maturation. Often we teach by example. We may suggest words or ways in which something might be done. Children follow our example, and use our words or ideas until they accomplish their task. In time, they need less help. It can be very satisfying for a child to learn and develop competency in something that once was challenging.

75. All God's people respond to Him in worship. When we believe in Him and trust Him, we are worshiping. Worship seems so familiar to us, yet it can intimidate us. Just watch what happens when someone is asked to volunteer to say a prayer in front of a group of people. Few may want to do it because they are afraid of saying the wrong thing or looking foolish. We don't need to be afraid as we worship our God. By His grace we will grow in confidence as He guides us in worship. This guidance can deepen our understanding and our relationship with our God. It can open new understanding to us as well.

Growing through Worship (Inform)

After reading the brief explanation, discuss the questions together.

76. Matthew 28:18–20 is the Great Commission of Jesus to His church. In verse 18 we find the invocation—the words used at the beginning of our worship service. When we hear these words, we are reminded of our own Baptism and of Jesus' promise to be with us always. We gather as the baptized and forgiven children of God. Because these words remind us of our Baptism, many Christians make the sign of the cross on themselves as they hear these words. This is a way of reminding ourselves that we too are baptized into Christ.

77. Matthew 15:22 records the words of a Canaanite woman and Mark 10:47 those of Bartimaeus, a blind man. Both people seek Jesus' blessing and healing, and so they cry out, "Lord, have mercy!" They knew that only Jesus could give them the healing they needed. Our worship uses these words in the part of the service known as the *Kyrie* (the Greek word for "Lord.") We, too, call out to God for His mercy. In one version of the Kyrie we simply pray "Lord have mercy, Christ have mercy, Lord have mercy." In other versions, brief prayers are said before the congregation responds, "Lord have mercy."

78. Luke 2:14 records the song of the angels at Jesus' birth: "Glory to God in the highest, and on earth peace to men on whom his favor rests." These words are ordinarily referred to as the *Gloria in Excelsis* (Latin for "Glory in the Highest"). When we sing them, we are joining the song of the angels in praising our Lord. Revelation 5:8–14 is repeated in the song "Worthy is Christ" (sometimes called "This is the Feast . . ."). In this passage we hear the song of heaven. Christ is praised because He is the redeemer of the world. St. John tells us that these words are sung by the heavenly angels, and echoed by every creature God has made. In other words, we sing them too!

79. We sing John 6:68 as part of the Alleluia verse (Divine Service II, *LW*). This sung verse precedes the reading of the Gospel for the day. Peter's words remind us that only Jesus has the words of eternal life. We hear that Word in the Gospel. This is not a mere recitation of an historical event. In the Gospel God again offers us His grace and eternal life.

80. In Psalm 51:10–12, we join David in praying that God would create a new heart within us. We are sinful people who need God to forgive our sin. We pray that He is merciful to us, grants us

71

forgiveness, and restores us to be His people. He does these things through Christ Jesus. By singing these words, we are reminded that our offerings, though they are a response to God's blessings, are nothing compared to what God has given us. His giving far exceeds the small gifts that we bring. Another passage of Scripture used as an offertory (usually during Lent) is "What Shall I Render to the Lord." This is based on Psalm 116:12–14, 17–19.

81. Matthew 6:9–13 contains the words of the Lord's Prayer (which is also found in Luke 11:1–4). We are not obligated to use these words. They are not the only acceptable words for prayer. However, they are an excellent model for prayer. This prayer covers a multitude of human needs. When we pray this prayer, we are again following the pattern of God's words in worship.

82. These verses are behind the song known as the *Sanctus* (the Latin word for "holy"). Like Isaiah, we are coming into God's presence. As sinners we would be consumed by His glory. Isaiah was spared when an angel took a coal from the heavenly altar, touched his lips with it, and said that he was forgiven. In Holy Communion, the body and blood of Christ are taken from the altar and placed on our lips. We are forgiven and able to enter God's presence. In singing the *Sanctus*, we add the words of Matthew 21:9, "Blessed is He who comes in the name of the Lord, Hosanna in the highest!" These words remind us that Christ, whose body and blood we are about to receive, is the holy and almighty God.

83. Jesus is the Lamb of God (in Latin, *Agnus Dei*) who takes away the sin of the world. He does this by sacrificing Himself on the cross for us. As Colossians 1:20 tells us, He has made "peace through His blood, shed on the cross." His sacrifice was sufficient to pay for the sins of the entire world.

84. Luke 2:29–32 is the *Nunc Dimittis* or Song of Simeon. God had promised Simeon that he would not die without seeing the Messiah with his own eyes. When Simeon was an old man, the baby Jesus was brought to the Temple. He responded by glorifying God. The promised Messiah had come, and he was ready to die and go to heaven. We may sing the same words after we commune. Just as God promised, we have seen and tasted the Lord. We have been blessed with His forgiveness and love. When God wills, we are prepared to enter His kingdom forever!

From the Heart (Connect)

85. Knowledge of God's Word is a blessing to His people. The more familiar we are with the Bible, the more use it will be in our lives. We ought to regularly hear and read God's Word for this very reason. It may surprise us, however, to see how much Scripture we have memorized through worship without even realizing it. There are other ways this can happen as well, but here is a strong example of how the Word might "dwell in us richly" (Colossians 3:16).

86. The repetition of texts does not mean that worship is always the same. We have looked at the repeating parts of worship—but these are only a portion of the Divine Service. The traditional Christian order of service is composed partly of these texts—but there are other elements that are changed every week. The Scripture readings, sermon, prayers, songs, and other elements are constantly changing. In this way, the service provides a balance of familiar and changing things each week. In addition, we have only looked at the words. These texts have been used by countless Christians for centuries. While they have all used the same words, they have not used the same music. Our own worship resources contain a number of different musical settings of these texts. There is no reason for these to be overly repetitious.

87. These are not Lutheran texts, nor are they German texts or even European texts. These classic liturgical texts belong to the whole church and have been in use for most of the history of the Christian church. These texts are freely used in other churches. Orthodox, Roman Catholics, Episcopalians and other liturgical churches use the same words that we do. In addition, many churches that do not ordinarily follow this common liturgical structure often use these texts and ideas in songs and other elements of worship. This is true because these are the words of Scripture. This is our common Christian heritage.

Digging Deeper (Vision)

88. Answers will vary.
89. Answers will vary.

Appendix on the Psalms in Worship

The following chart will introduce you to some of the liturgical uses of the psalms from the Old Testament.

Ritual Acts	References	Notes
Pilgrimage	Psalm 120–134	Israelites were required to make annual pilgrimages to the sanctuary. Singing psalms was part of the journey.
Procession	Psalm 24:7, 9; 48; 118:19–20; 132	Psalm 132 may have been used as a reenactment of the moving of the ark of the covenant (2 Samuel 6).
Dancing	Psalm 149:3; 150:4. See Exodus 15:20; Judges 21:16–24; 2 Samuel 6:14, 16.	Dance was not an individualistic action, as in modern times, but a liturgical act. (e.g., Moses' anger at the dancing before the golden calf; the Israelites were performing a ritual dance as an act of idol worship.) Israelites probably used ritual dances in their processions to the sanctuary.
Entrance Liturgies	Psalm 15:1–5; 24:3–6	The priests or Levites may have asked the questions found in these psalms. The people may have voiced the responses before entering into the worship area.

Invocation	Psalm 33:1; 111:1; 113:1; 146–150	These psalms seem to have opened a service of praise, prayer, or sacrifice. They invite the congregation to participate with the priests and Levites.
Versicle and Response	Psalm 124; 129; 136	Psalm 124:1 and 129:1 command, "Let Israel say." This may be a cue from a priest or Levite for the congregation to recite a response.
Choirs	Psalm 4; 5; 6; etc.	Many psalms were written for the "director of music" or "choir director."
Ceremonial Washings	Psalm 26:6; 51:7	Washing was a regular part of service at the temple because of the animal sacrifices, but it was also an expression of forgiveness and purity.
Offering	Psalm 66:13–15	The Law of Moses does not prescribe words to accompany the sacrificial acts of the priests. The psalms seem to serve as the "words of institution" for the sacrifices.
Lament/ Fasting	Psalm 44; 60; 74; 79; etc.	In times of national crisis and perhaps also during festivals, Israelites used lament psalms and fasted.

4 Maccabees, a Jewish intertestamental book, remarks that the psalms were used in the home (18:9–10, 15). Parents were responsible for teaching psalms to their children.

Appendix of Lutheran Teaching

The Augsburg Confession of 1530

Philip Melanchthon, a lay associate of Dr. Martin Luther, wrote the Augsburg Confession to clarify for Emperor Charles V just what Lutherans believed. Melanchthon summarized Lutheran teaching from the Bible and addressed the controversies of the day. This confession remains a standard of Lutheran teaching.

Article XXIV 34

Now, forasmuch as the Mass is such a giving of the Sacrament, we hold one communion every holy-day, and, if any desire the Sacrament, also on other days, when it is given to such as ask for it.

Apology of the Augsburg Confession

Philip Melanchthon, a lay associate of Dr. Martin Luther, wrote the apology to clarify for Emperor Charles V just what Lutherans believed. Melanchthon summarized Lutheran teaching from the Bible and addressed the controversies of his day. This apology remains a standard of Lutheran teaching.

Article III 189

The worship and divine service of the Gospel is to receive from God gifts; on the contrary, the worship of the Law is to offer and present our gifts to God. We can, however, offer nothing to God unless we have first been reconciled and born again. This passage, too, brings the greatest consolation, as the chief worship of the Gospel is to wish to receive remission of sins, grace, and righteousness.

Article XV 51

And nevertheless we teach that in these matters the use of liberty is to be so controlled that the inexperienced may not be offended, and, on account of the abuse of liberty, may not become more hostile to the true doctrine of the Gospel, or that without a reasonable cause nothing in customary rites be changed, but that, in order to cherish harmony, such old customs be observed as can be observed without sin or without great inconvenience.

The Large Catechism

The Large Catechism of Dr. Martin Luther sprang from a series of sermons he preached to help his congregation understand the basic teachings of the Bible. It serves as a companion for pastors and teachers as they explain Luther's Small Catechism.

Part II 66

Although they believe in, and worship, only one true God, yet know not what His mind toward them is, and cannot expect any love or blessing from Him . . . for they have not the Lord Christ, and, besides, are not illumined and favored by the gifts of the Holy Ghost.

Part V 47

That is true, yet it is not written that we should never do so. Yea, just because He speaks the words, *As oft as ye do it*, it is nevertheless implied that we should do it often; and it is added for the reason that He wishes to have the Sacrament free, not limited to special times, like the Passover of the Jews, which they were obliged to eat only once a year, and that just upon the fourteenth day of the first full moon in the evening, and which they must not vary a day. As if He would say by these words: I institute a Passover or Supper for you which you shall enjoy not only once a year, just upon this evening, but often, when and where you will, according to every one's opportunity and necessity, bound to no place or appointed time.

Formula of Concord

Following Luther's death in 1546, confusion disrupted the Lutheran churches. Some wished to compromise on matters of doctrine in order to attain greater peace and unity with Calvinists and Roman Catholics. Others claimed to be true Lutherans but strayed from Luther's teaching. In 1576 Elector August of Saxony called a conference to clarify the issues. The result was the Formula of Concord (*concord* means "unity"), published in 1580.

Epitome X 5

Nevertheless, that herein all frivolity and offense should be avoided, and special care should be taken to exercise forbearance towards the weak in faith. 1 Corinthians 8, 9; Romans 14, 13.

Epitome X 6

We believe, teach, and confess that in time of persecution, when a plain [and steadfast] confession is required of us, we should not yield to the enemies in regard to such adiaphora.… For in such a case it is no longer a question concerning adiaphora, but concerning the truth of the Gospel, concerning [preserving] Christian liberty, and concerning sanctioning open idolatry, as also concerning the prevention of offense to the weak in the faith [how care should be taken lest idolatry be openly sanctioned and the weak in faith be offended]; in which we have nothing to concede, but should plainly confess and suffer on that account what God sends, and what He allows the enemies of His Word to inflict upon us.

Glossary

adiaphora. Literally "indifferent things." Things that God has neither commanded nor forbidden such as certain traditions for worship.

Antinomianism. The view that Christians are free of all moral law.

catechism. From the Greek word meaning "oral instruction," used by St. Paul in Galatians 6:6. A catechism is a book, usually in question-and-answer format, containing basic instruction.

corporate worship. People worshiping together in a group ("corporate" comes from the Latin word, *corpus*, "body").

creed. From the Latin word *credo,* "I believe." Creeds are summary confessions of faith used by the vast majority of Christians. They developed at a time when most people could not read and needed a memorable rule of faith.

Divine Service. A translation of a German term for worship, *Gottesdienst.*

filioque. Literally, "and the Son." This phrase was added to the Nicene Creed in the West to emphasize that the Holy Spirit proceeds from the Father and the Son. The Eastern churches have never accepted this statement, but insist that the Spirit proceeds only from the Father.

Gloria in Excelsis. Latin for "Glory to God in the highest," sung by the angels (Luke 2:14). The Gloria is sung in the liturgy to praise God for salvation through Jesus.

Gospel. The message of Christ's death and resurrection for the forgiveness of sins. The Holy Spirit works through the Gospel to create faith and convert people.

Judaizers. A group in the early hurch that wished to impose Jewish practices such as circumcision on the Gentiles. Judaizers viewed obedience to the Old Testament Law as necessary for salvation.

justification. God declares sinners to be just or righteous for Christ's sake; that is, God has imputed or charged our sins to Christ and He imputes or credits Christ's righteousness to us.

Kyrie. Greek for "Lord." The Kyrie is a prayer based on biblical pleas for God's help (e.g., Mark 10:47).

Law. God's will which shows people how they should live (e.g., the Ten Commandments) and condemns their failure. The preaching of the Law is the cause of contrition.

lectionary. From the Latin word for "reading." A collection of texts for public reading.

means of grace. The means by which God gives us the forgiveness, life, and salvation, won by the death and resurrection of Christ: the Gospel, Baptism, and the Lord's Supper.

Nunc Dimmitis. From the Latin for "Now dismiss," the opening words of Simeon's song in Luke 2:29. The Nunc Dimmitis is sung after the congregation receives the Lord's Supper.

Offertory. A song accompanying the collecting of the offering.

polemical. From the Greek word for "battle." The term describes conversation or writing that attacks and refutes.

Sacrament. Literally, something sacred. In the Lutheran church, a Sacrament is a sacred act that (1) was instituted by God, (2) has a visible element, and (3) offers the forgiveness of sins earned by Christ. The Sacraments include Baptism, the Lord's Supper, and also absolution (if one counts the pastor as the visible element).

sanctification. The spiritual growth that follows justification by grace through faith in Christ.

Sanctus. Latin for "Holy," from the song of the angels in Isaiah 6.

vocation. From the Latin word for "calling." A person's occupation or duties before God. For example, a person may serve as a father, a husband, and an engineer. Each "calling" comes with different responsibilities.